Giacinto Auriti

THE LAND OF UTOPIA
The answer to Ezra Pound's five questions

I0409294

Introduction by Marino Solfanelli

English translation and editing by Marco Saba

First English edition to celebrate the **"Centenary of the birth of prof. Giacinto Auriti: 10 October 1923 - 10 October 2023"**

First Italian edition: October 2003

INTRODUCTION

"I am a farmer who became a university professor as a hobby". Giacinto Auriti

Ezra Loomis Pound (Hailey, Idaho, 1885 – Venice, Italy, 1972) and Giacinto Auriti (Guardiagrele, October 10, 1923 – Rome, August 11, 2006), the peasant poet and jurist. The American – who chooses Italy as his adopted homeland – and the Italian from Abruzzo. Apparently different characters, by origin and culture, but united by an indissoluble bond: the search for the truth at all costs. Ezra Pound, the American poet fascinated by European culture, by the Middle Ages of "Father", in which he discovered a universal reality from which he drew inspiration for the "*Canti Pisani*" (poem he wrote during his imprisonment in the American concentration camp of Coltano, in the province of Pisa, where he was locked up in a cage). It is the price that he was forced to pay precisely for having loved Italy and observed with interest the awakening of Europe.

The Poet felt the need for a renewal that was not limited to a sterile rhetorical exercise of youth, but which constituted the basis of a life lived and not vegetated: therefore interior cleansing, elimination of the false myths of ideologies that were substitutes for ideals: «*As long as you have not clarified your thought within yourself, you cannot communicate it to others. / Until you have brought order within yourself, you cannot be an element of order in the party.*»

Giacinto Auriti elaborates a new philosophical theory on the judgment of value "as a relationship between phases of time" which will lead him to the discovery of the "induced value" of money.

The two characters, who have never met, are united by a prophecy contained in lines 101-102 of the Inferno, where the poet, after speaking of the she-wolf who blocked his path, announced the coming of a *Veltro* "who will cause you to die in pain." The "wolf" for Pound is usurocracy, against which he fights for a new concept of life. Work and usury is the title of a collection of essays written after the Second World War, on the title page we read "*Bellum cano perenne*, between usury and the man who wants to do a good job". Pound understood that money is not a commodity but the expression of an agreement, a convention, whereby credit must be entrusted not to banks but to the State, which guarantees it with the honesty and work of its citizens . «*The treasure of a nation is its honesty.*» And in the "Cantos" he expresses his thoughts on usury: «*With usury no one has a solid house / of squared and smooth stone / to decorate its façade, / (…) / Carrion crapulates / guests of usury.* » (Against

Usury, Canto XLV) Ezra Pound asks five questions that no one had ever answered: money, credit, interest, usury and circulation; Giacinto Auriti gives, in this essay, precise answers. An ideal continuity that unites them in the school of heretical economists.

"Those who create the value of money – says Giacinto Auriti – are not those who print it but the people who accept it as a means of payment", however, they are the bankers, the great usurers who appropriate the monetary value, using it as a means of domination and imposing debt seigniorage on humanity. And here is the ingenious solution to the problem: Popular ownership of money, which returns to the people the ill-gotten gains of the monetary values that it creates. The hope is that governments will manage the monetary issue and distribute the profits, as a right of citizenship, to all citizens.

The two scholars, the American poet, born to Quaker and Puritan parents, and the Abruzzo jurist, traditionalist and Catholic, are both gratuitously opposed by the fashionable culture, plagiarized in the mystifying meaning of the lords of usury. Ezra Pound, in our opinion, never detaches himself sentimentally from peasant America, but is fascinated by the creative and innovative force of the war of blood against gold, which creates new flourishing cities where malaria, pestilence and death once thrived.

Among the many followers of Auriti's theories there are also left-wing men, who by virtue of those theories are beginning to hope for a future freed from the seigniorage of great usury. As Auriti himself recalls, in *Work and Usury* Pound writes: «*last September 10th I passed along the Via Salaria past Fara Sabina and after a certain time I entered the republic of Utopia, a placid country lying outside the present geography.*» In a note Pound adds: «*I had written: "Utopia, a placid country lying eighty years east of Fara Sabina".*» Since a spatial and a temporal dimension coincide in this sentence, it should be highlighted that SIMEC (SIMbolo EConometrico a Valore Indotto, Induced Value Econometric Symbol), defined by monetarists as poundian money, property of the bearer (and not of the bank), eighty years after the birth of Fascism (1921-22). And Guardiagrele is east of Fara Sabina.

Pound's prophecy duly came true. It could be the sign of blood's revenge against gold. On the margin of the SIMEC there is an ancient phrase from Abruzzo wisdom: "*Non bene pro toto libertas venditur auro*" (It is not good to sell one's freedom for all the gold in the world) which echoes Pound's teaching: «The treasure of a nation is its honesty." We're starting to hope...

Marino Solfanelli

EZRA POUND AND THE ROMANCE OF THE TWENTIETH CENTURY

«The nineteenth century, infamous century of usury...»[1]
"I fell asleep under the Sabine stars, (...) marveling at the distance that had passed between the world of the twentieth century and that of serenity..."[2].

With these two lapidary sentences Pound expresses the causal link between two centuries of history: *Post hoc ergo propter hoc* (after this, therefore for this). The advent of usurocracy is the cause of the anguish that characterizes the spiritual climate of our time. It is no coincidence that in the language born in American mercantile practice, usury is defined with the term "danger". Danger is incompatible with serenity. In the century of usury all peoples have become poor because they have been indebted for a value equal to all their money since 1694 – as Pound intuited – the date of establishment of the Bank of England. From these few words the greatness of Pound's intuition emerges. The entire culture of the twentieth century is permeated with romanticism. The great problems that trouble the generation are felt and suffered: the philosophical and scientific awareness to solve them is lacking. *«What has been missing in Italy, especially among practical people, among industrialists, both large and small, among merchants, and not only among small merchants, is the vision of the loan sharking process, the knowledge of the relationship and of the relationships between the business, between the management of a productive or commercial company, and the world monetary system, operating not in the short term, not in periods of three months or three years, but in the long run, over centuries and half-centuries, always with the same plan: to profit. And always with the same mechanisms: that is, creating debts to exploit the interest, and monopolies to be able to vary the price of everything, including the price of the different units of the different currencies of different nations.»*[3] Pound thus highlighted that money is the great cultural gap in the Romano-Christian tradition. Even though he declared himself a fascist, he highlighted the cultural limits of Fascism, common to all the romantic movements of the twentieth century. Romanticism means feeling the problems of your generation more with your blood than with your brain. With a humility equal to his love for the truth, he says: *«... we ask what money, credit, interest, usury is.*
«Before discussing a monetary policy, a monetary reform, a monetary revolution, we must be very sure of the nature of money.
«The enemy is (our) ignorance.

---

1   Ezra Pound, Work and Usury, Milan 1972, p. 25.
2   E. Pound, op. cit.
3   E. Pound, op. cit., p. 54.

At the beginning of the nineteenth century, John Adams (*pater patriae*) saw that the defects and errors of the American government derived not so much from the corruption of the personnel, but from an ignorance of money, credit and their circulation. *"We're at the same point."*[4] And we still ask ourselves today.

Are we at the same point? We think not. In fact, we are now in a position to be able to give a comprehensive answer to the five questions posed by Pound: *"What is money, credit, interest, usury, (...) and circulation"*. We are convinced that by answering these five questions we will fill the cultural gap that caused the collapse of the Catholic monarchies of Old Europe and the defeat of 20th century romanticism. To this end, it seems essential to make a brief introduction to define value and distinguish between the physiology and pathology of value judgments.

VALUE IS A RELATIONSHIP
BETWEEN PHASES OF TIME...

... like this for example: a pen has value because it is expected to write, the knife has value because it is expected to cut, the coin has value because it is expected to buy.

The value is therefore the ratio between the moment of prediction and the foreseen moment. Since time, as Kant said, is the I that presents itself as reality as an ongoing capacity to notice, predict and remember – and the I present in its vital continuity is the constant of time – we explain why, not Since time without life or "value without life" is conceivable, there is no wealth in a world of the dead.

The error of the romantic schools lies essentially in the fact that they conceived value as a property of matter, that is, as a dimension of space. Space coincides only with the present: everything else is time. So Pound, despite having understood the problem, was unable to solve it because economic culture ignored (and still ignores) the phenomenon of forecasting activity in which the value judgment itself is realized. This cultural limit is denounced by Pound in a significant sentence: «... *I welcome with relief F. Ritter's tendency to talk about money not in terms of "finance" and "economy" but in terms of grain and fertilizer.*»[5] The expression is a significant example of the romantic

---

4   E. Pound, op. cit., p. 20.
5   E. Pound, op. cit., p. 56.

culture of the twentieth century: very noble and ingenious in identifying and criticizing the evil tyranny of great usury, but incapable of constructively indicating the remedies. If Ritter's theory were true there would be no difference between barter and buying and selling. Only after the discovery of the induced value is it possible to distinguish the value of the measurement (money) from the measured value (grain and fertilizer).

Once it has been highlighted that value is a relationship between phases of time, the distinction must be made between the instrumental phase which concerns the object (e.g. the pen) and the hedonistic phase which concerns the subject (e.g. writing with the pen) . This distinction between the objective moment and the subjective moment in which the physiology of value is realized is obviously based on the dualistic conception of philosophy of knowledge (Aristotelian-Thomist), in which the object is distinguished from the subject.

Since the past and the future do not coincide with the present ego (which is the constant of time) they are the object of memory and prediction, i.e. the object of value judgement. When the value judgment is built on the philosophical basis of Hegelian monism (in which the object is confused with the subject due to the reduction of reality to the idea of reality in the so-called idealism), the objective instrumental moment becomes immanent, with the subjective hedonistic one, with the consequence of personifying the instrument. Thus was born the concept of society without human content, the legal ghost that characterized the advent of capitalism: of which the usurocracy intuited by Pound is a constitutive and essential part. In fact, with the confusion between the instrumental or functional moment (prerogative of the organ) and the hedonistic moment (prerogative of the social community) the great cultural disease of the organic representation of the hedonistic moment of value was born. As if to say – referring to *Menenius Agrippa*'s apologue – that, while the people take on the function of being hungry, the government takes on that of eating on behalf of the people.

Ownership (even of money) – which is the juridically protected enjoyment of goods and therefore relevant to the second time phase of value – is taken away from the human person and attributed to legal ghosts. Instrumental subjectivities, operational tools of capitalism, have become the screens of the great mangers. Constitutional state, socialist state, joint-stock company, state corporation, bank, multinational, etc. they are all concepts of society without human content, that is, tools that have distorted the ethical foundations of traditional organic society. It is no coincidence that all banks are joint-stock company ("S.p.A.", Italian for *Società per Azioni*) Since it is unthinkable and absurd to serve an instrument, the rule of serving typical of organic society has been replaced by that of serving typical of instrumental subjectivity. The principle of "it pays to be right" has consequently been replaced by the principle of "what is right is right". It is no coincidence that the phenomenon of *tangentopoli*[6] does not only constitute a statistical expression of an increase in political delinquency, but manifests, in its grandeur, the sign of the times of decadence we are experiencing. Having said this, let's answer Ezra Pound's five questions.

1-2 MONEY AND CIRCULATION

Money was comprehensively defined by Aristotle as a measure of value. In every sentence there are always two meanings: one explicit and the other implicit. The limitation of monetarists lies in the fact that they limited themselves to considering only the explicit meaning of Aristotle's definition, "measure of value" and ignored the implicit one: "value of measure".

In fact, each unit of measurement necessarily has the quality corresponding to what it must measure. Just as the meter has the quality of length because it measures length, the coin has the quality of value because it measures value. So money is not only the measure of value, but also the value of the measure which is purchasing power.

Since every unit of measurement is a convention and every convention is a legal case, money is a legal case. Therefore, the raw material for manufacturing money is the same that is used to produce legal cases: spiritual form and reality, *i.e.* symbol and monetary convention. In short, the symbol acquires monetary value for the simple fact that we agree that it has it. The forecast of others' behavior as a condition of one's own, leads everyone to accept money for goods because they expect to be able to give, in turn, money for goods. The birth of monetary value, even in the symbol of zero cost[7], led Pythagoras to define monetary value as the "magic of number". By number we meant measurement because every measurement is a numerical expression: so much so that we normally speak of a "unit" of measurement.

---

6   The political-administrative system in which it is normal practice to give and receive bribes
     (then, par excellence, the Italian bribe scandal and the world that is implicated in it).
7   Paper money created at pure printing cost.

To explain the mystery of the magic of number we have applied the fundamental principle of the "circularity of sciences" whereby, when it is not possible to explain a phenomenon within the scientific category in which it occurs, we must resort to a different scientific category by applying the principle by analogy. With this method we discovered legal induction using the experience of physical induction. Just as in the dynamo mechanical energy is transformed into electrical energy, so in money the value of a convention, that is, of a spiritual reality, is transformed into a real good object of ownership. Here time is objectified by induction in a more intense way than happens in other legal cases.

While as a rule the peculiar instrumentality of each rule consists in the typical "regulatory prediction", the function of money is not limited to the conventional (*i.e.* normative) measurement of the value of economic goods alone, but constitutes, itself, a good subject to exchange because it incorporates by legal induction the "value of the measure". In the monetary case, the formal element of the symbol does not have the sole purpose of manifesting the convention, but by giving the bearer the expectation of "being able to purchase", *i.e.* the purchasing power, it incorporates the "value of the measure" and thus becomes a new good, completely autonomous and different from those measured, so much so that it constitutes its equivalent in the negotiation of the sale.

This argument could not be considered by Pound because he did not know that value is "time" and not "space", *i.e.* prediction and not commodity. Just as in the dynamo the alternation of the positive and negative poles in the rotation of the armature causes the electromagnetic field which generates electrical energy, so in the monetary convention the succession of phases of the circulation of money in one's own hands and those of others similarly determines the alternation of the " I" with the "not I", of 'mine' with 'yours', which generates, by legal induction, monetary value.

Just as, in the physical industry, electrical energy is born when the rotation of the dynamo begins, similarly the monetary value is born when it is issued in the hands of the acceptor because it provides for its further transfer and circulation in the legal industry. Just as in the dynamo, increasing the speed of rotation increases the quantity of electrical energy, so increasing the speed of circulation of money increases its induced value, *i.e.* purchasing power. On this principle, investment banks create unlimited quantities of value, attributing the speed of light to bank deposits by transferring them from one continent to another with the electronic impulses of computers. The phenomenon was defined by the

Governor of the Bank of Italy as "transnational deposits that escape the control of central banks".

Since the induced value is caused by the circulation of money, similarly to the electrical energy caused by the rotation of the dynamo, lacking scientific awareness of the phenomenon, to express the concept, governor Fazio linked the word "deposit" which has a static meaning, with the term "transnational" which has a dynamic meaning. He thus proposed an irrational definition of the induced value because it was expressed with two incompatible terms.

In conclusion, money is not only the product of a convention, but of a conventional activity which, in its continuity, creates "purchasing power" by induction in a case of legal sociology. The currency that does not circulate is a mere symbol, it is not money. The monetary symbol can take on all possible forms of legal cases. Just as the red and green light of the traffic light is a form of legal rules, because they allow and prohibit transit, so the monetary symbol can be created, by convention, in the light of the computer.

To explain the difference between law and legal sociology it is enough to give an elementary example: the "purchase contract" is a legal case; "buyer and seller bound by contract" is a case of legal sociology. It is within this second case that induced value arises and exists in its continuity. Just as the electric current is caused by the rotation that alternates positive and negative poles of the generating elements, so the self and the other, the self and the non-self, are the juridical poles within which the induced value arises. Like electrical energy

Electricity is not born if the dynamo does not turn, so monetary value is not born if money does not circulate in the trading activity of the market. Money is living law.

3 – CREDIT

The credit has a value commensurate with that of the service covered by the credit. The currency has a value commensurate with the numerical amount of the units of measurement of value represented in it. It is a pure legal value caused by social convention both in its essence and in its amount.

Credit, such as the bill of exchange is extinguished upon payment. Money continues to circulate after each transaction because, like any unit of measurement, it is a good with repeated utility.

Today's monetary schools, ignoring the distinction between credit value and induced value, have defined money with the absurd formula of "debt and/or bad credit" to justify its existence and repeated use. The result was the absurd declaration placed on the banknotes (e.g. Lire One Thousand payable on demand to the bearer. Signed: The Governor of the Bank of Italy) conceived as false bills of exchange. Since the value of the credit is given by its collectability, this currency should have no value so it should be indifferent to us whether we have money in our pockets or not.

The monetary convention is so much more important than that of language that the paper declaration here imposes an interpretation that is even incompatible with the literal one. In fact, everyone knows well that the banknote, despite being a false bill of exchange, is real money. Only on these premises can it be explained why Paterson founded the Bank of England in 1694 on the rule of lending the bank's (false) bills instead of gold. Since the value of the bill of exchange is caused by the debtor's promise, by passing off money under the guise of a bill of exchange, the governor arrogated to himself the right to issue money which he appropriated because he lent it at the time of issuance. And lending money is the owner's prerogative. Therefore the governor is a false debtor, but the true owner of the money. In this way the currency becomes the property of the bank which issues it and lends it to the citizens. It should instead be owned by citizens and be credited to them as citizenship income.

The bank is therefore a criminal association that passes off its crimes as a business for the victims. Once it has been established that the currency is a false bill of exchange, it is explained why the Central Bank reports the issued currency to the liabilities side of the balance sheet, falsifying it.

4 – INTEREST

It is the price of using money. By analogy we can say that it is like the rent that the tenant pays to the owner for the use of the apartment. The difference lies in the fact that while in renting the ownership of the rented object remains in the hands of the lessor, in renting money, *i.e.* in lending, ownership passes into the hands of the tenant (*i.e.* the debtor) because the enjoyment of the money it lies essentially in its expendability, that is, in being able to transfer ownership during the sale.

Closely linked to the issue of interest is that of the rarity of the coin. In fact, the amount of interest is functionally linked to the rarity of the coin. To date, no school has managed to provide a valid scientific justification of the rarity limit on which to plan the issuance of money. This is the reason why there was no possibility of establishing a criterion of technical discretion to scientifically justify and regulate the duty of the monetary function. This gap in monetary science finds its significant expression in an answer given by Einaudi to those who asked him what the law of rarity was: *"The rarity of gold has been replaced by the wisdom of governors"*. These words, in their obvious absurdity, are the symptom of the now consolidated habit in the practice of attributing to the governor of the central bank not an organic function, as it should be, but the most absolute, uncontrollable and unquestionable arbitrariness because it is carried out by a "wise " par excellence, even if in violation of criminal laws.

The solution to the problem is therefore only possible if we understand that money must be rare because it measures the value of economic goods which are such because they are rare, *i.e.* limited in quantity compared to the extent of needs. Since each unit of measurement must have the quality corresponding to what it must measure, just as the meter has the quality of length because it measures length, the coin must have the quality of rarity because the goods whose value it measures are rare.

When the coin was made of gold, the serious flaw was rigid and uncontrollable rarity. With the advent of nominal money, rarity was programmed not according to objective social interests, but those of usury.

In other words, given that the market price is not only the index of the value of the goods, but also of the market saturation point – whereby the market is saturated when the price tends to coincide with the production costs – only when this tendency occurs, we must desist both from the production of goods and from the issuing of money.

This market normalization is only possible if the currency is declared bearer-owned and without reserve since its issue. However, when it is issued on loan and with a reserve, the market is dominated by usury for two reasons:

a) because, at the time of issue, it becomes the property of the bank that issues it by lending, *i.e.* by charging the market with a debt which is not owed of which he can arbitrarily request the repayment in times and quantities unquestionably established by the Governor of the Central Bank (a S.p.A., a private for-profit company);

b) because, once it has been demonstrated that the currency has an induced and non-credit value, the reserve serves only as a pretext to have the justification of limiting the issuance of the currency to the (presumed and arbitrarily established) amount of the reserve.

This is the reason why, at the time of issue, the Central Bank, in order to maintain control over the monetary values created by citizens (and which should therefore be credited to them), issues them by lending them, that is, by charging them in the most gigantic scam of all times. Great usury has thus transformed people from owners into debtors of their own money. Only on these premises can the note that appeared in the Hazard Circular in 1862, recalled by Pound, be explained: «*The great debt that our friends, the capitalists of Europe, will try to raise from this war, will be used to manipulate the (monetary) circulation. We cannot allow state notes (greenbacks) to circulate because we cannot regulate them (i.e. their issuance, etc.)*», as they are not burdened with debt[8].

Pound is right when he states: «*Usury sharks provoke wars to create debts.*»[9] Since we know that the same currency today is a debt because it is issued by central banks only by lending it, Pound's sentence must be completed thus: "*to pay other debts in a chronic, unavoidable insolvency*".

Today we have proof that war is not only the means to preserve and increase debts (not owed), but also murder, to avoid their extinction (with state notes). Recently in the magazine *Chiesa Viva*[10] under the title *"The assassination of*

---

8   E. Pound, op. cit., p. 14.
9   E. Pound, op. cit., p. 14.
10 "Chiesa Viva", n. 338, Brescia, April 2002, p. 15.

J.F. Kennedy" the true reason for the historic crime is documented. After the President's assassination, Vice President J.B. Johnson, as soon as he assumed the office of President, ordered the withdrawal of all the banknotes printed by Kennedy with his executive order 11110 of 4 June 1963. These banknotes no longer bore the writing "FEDERAL RESERVE NOTE", but "**UNITED STATES NOTE**"(!!!) as emerges from the two images reproduced in the article.[11]

Therefore Kennedy had understood that the hegemony of usury was based on the rule, born with the central bank, of "issuing money by lending it to the national community" which, creating its value with acceptance, must, instead, be its owner from the moment of emission. This is why everyone can lend money, except those who issue it.

Issuing money by lending it is the seigniorage of the great usury which was born in 1694 with the Bank of England denounced by Pound as *".... criminal association..."*[12]. However, Pound is wrong when, commenting on Paterson's words, he limits this usurious withdrawal to 60%. The famous phrase of William Paterson, founder of the Bank of England: *«The bank benefits from the interest on all the money it creates from nothing»* [13], which appears unscrupulously sincere, in fact hides the most important part of the truth because it is not true that the bank is enriched only by the interest, but also and above all by the money itself, whose value – as we have seen – is not created by the bank, but by the community. Therefore the cost of money is not only 60 %, but also by a further 200% because a credit (+100%) is transformed into a debt (-100%) without any compensation!

Banking charity is stronger than Christian charity. Christian charity teaches us to forgive debts. Banking charity even teaches how to pay debtors. Central banks which, by lending what they owe, collect their debts as creditors.

---

11 Translator's note: Legal Tender State notes: in the appendix you will find both Kennedy's Executive Order and the Italian Law inspired by it and passed in 1966 by the Moro government for the 500 lire notes issued as legal tender state note.

12 E. Pound, op. cit., p. 10.

13 E. Pound, op. cit., p. 19.

5 – USURY

The Usury understood by Pound is seigniorage. We cannot understand why Pound declared himself a fascist if we do not start from Mussolini's fundamental message: *"The war of blood against gold"*. And we cannot understand this message if we do not start from the fundamental conception of the "ethical state" in which Catholicism is "State Religion".

The absolute incompatibility between the ethical state and the democratic state lies in the fact that in the former the foundation is the "thirst for justice", in the latter ethics is a variant because the law of numbers (the will of the majority) is, by its nature, finalistically neutral and modifiable with cultural strategies of domination (mass media).

The most important phenomenon that occurred with the French Revolution was not the constitutional charter, but the central bank with the simultaneous replacement of gold coins with nominal money. This was not a simple change in the product structure of the symbol, but the replacement of one legal case with another.

When the coin was gold, the bearer was its owner; with nominal money, he has unwittingly become its debtor. All nominal money is issued by central banks by lending it: therefore all money in circulation is burdened with debt to central banks. By leveraging the conditioned reflex caused by the centuries-old habit of always giving a consideration for having money, the central banks have induced all the peoples of the world to accept their own currency at the time of issue, with the consideration for the debt, *i.e.* on loan, in **the biggest scam of all time, which went unnoticed because it was too obvious.**

So if someone wanted to pay a debt of money with money, it is as if he wanted to pay another debt with a debt. In the long run he is forced to pay an undue debt with his own capital and the income from his work. This is **the seigniorage of great usury** by which man is placed at a lower rank than that of the beast. In fact, the beast does not have property, but not even debt. Debt (nominal) money is Satan's masterpiece. The rule is usually that there are no good or bad tools, but only good or bad ways to use them. With debt money, whoever accepts it is cheated, for the sole fact that he accepts it, because he is simultaneously expropriated and indebted because he accepts **a loan of his own money** and **creates the value of it by accepting it** and is **simultaneously expropriated and indebted** because he accepts the loan at the time of issue.

This undue debt, born, as we have seen, with an initial cost of 200%, circulates in the anguish of inevitable insolvency. It is the great usury born with the pound and the Bank of England in 1694.

The proof of this lies in the fact that, once upon a time, people worked for a profit. Today he works to pay off debts. Suicide due to insolvency has become a social disease that has no precedent in history: *"...usury is worse than the plague..."*: Pound is right. The expression he proposed of "usurocracy"; it shakes from its foundations the *communis opinio* which has placed the rule of law of the liberal school in the Olympus of definitive and untouchable concepts. *"We ask the liberals (who are not all loan sharks): why are the loan sharks all liberals?"*[14]

That today the politician is – as Pound said – the "banker's waiter", emerges from the obvious consideration that, if the governor of the Central Bank and the Head of Government are compared, the former can grant or deny in loan all the money he wants, the second can only ask for it or not ask for it, only on loan. It is therefore obvious that the second is the first's waiter, but not because he is servile, but because the rules of the game do not allow otherwise.

CONCLUSION

In conclusion, the solution to the problems brought to the attention of the world by Pound lies in claiming, in favor of every people, the ownership of their money. The monetary revolution of the Bank of England transformed the bearer's property-money (gold) into nominal money (bearer's debt and bank property). The counter-revolution must transform debt money into money owned by the bearer (not by the bank), without reserve (like gold), with a symbol of zero cost (like paper). Only in this way will it be possible to restore to every man the legal dignity that he deserves, free him from the anguish of inevitable insolvency due to debts not owed and allow him, finally, to live new times on a human scale. The reader should not be surprised by our admission of having deduced our answers to Pound from his teaching, because Pound not only gave us the premonition of monetary truth (the induced value of money), but also and above all the great ethical teaching of the search for truth at any cost.

---

14   E. Pound, op. cit., p. 15.

Post Scriptum

GUARDIAGRELE, THE COUNTRY OF UTOPIA

Marino Solfanelli, on whose shoulders the responsibility for the publication of this short essay falls, has challenged us to explain why Ezra Pound declared himself a fascist. The need for this clarification emerges from the fact that, in the *communis opinio*, this Poundian gesture is judged as confession of a sin. The cultural plagiarism planned by the winners managed to pass off an advantage as a flaw. Since in politics what is not manifested does not exist (and manifestation has a cost), those who paid the piper of history have chosen the music of the "false truth": The usurers, masters of money, have officially and authoritatively passed off, for democracy, usurocracy.

If by democracy we mean sovereign people, then the people must not only have political sovereignty, but also monetary sovereignty in an integral democracy which is based on the "thirst for justice" (like the Roman plebiscite) and not on the law of number which is purposefully and ethically neutral. Experience has in fact taught us that the majority is often achieved not by those who love the people, but by those who have the money to buy it.

The word "democracy" which was born seven centuries earlier in Greece, is not used once in the Gospel and the only time that "democracy" is applied in the Gospel, the people send Christ to the cross and free Barabbas so that, according to democratic ethics, we should praise Barabbas and condemn Christ.

Democracy is, at most, a code of procedure, not a code of honor. Pound had understood that when Mussolini declared and promoted the war of blood against gold he was absolutely right. He felt this message of justice so deeply that he declared himself a fascist with superhuman moral strength, recognizing as an American citizen, in time of war, that his homeland was fighting on the wrong side. Fate had assigned him the land where he was to be born.

When he was able to personally choose where to live and die, he preferred the land, defeated yes, but on the side of blood: rather than remaining on his side, although victorious, but on the side of gold. In a precious and prophetic note he says: *«Last September 10th I passed along the Via Salaria, beyond Fara Sabina and after a certain time I entered the republic of Utopia, a placid country lying outside the present geography.»*[15] And then he adds: «I had written: "Utopia, a

_____
15 E. Pound, op. cit., p. 7.

16

placid country lying eighty years east of Fara Sabina" (...)»[16] . The reader should not be shocked if we dare to think that the town of Utopia, prophesied by Pound, is Guardiagrele. It is in fact to the east of Fara Sabina and in that same town, eighty years later, was born what was defined not by chance, the poundian currency, property of the bearer and not of the bank, without debt and without reserves: the Simec. At this point it might seem that the writer is a fascist citizen of Guardiagrele. He is from Guardiagrele yes, but not a fascist because this definition is "too little".

The war of blood against gold ineluctably continues and we do not want to continue to lose. When the banker Lord Bennet says to Pound: *"It took us twenty years to beat Napoleon, five years will be enough to beat fascism"*, he demonstrated his cultural (not moral) superiority because history proved him right. Mussolini couldn't win the war because he didn't understand that the enemy to beat was the usurers' gold: the debt currency of the Bank of England. The popular ownership of money is the great revenge in the game of history that faithfully unites us with the heroes, of every political party or colour, who fought on the same frontier against great usury.

We will transform all the peoples of the world from debtors to owners of money, simply because this idea was born. Sociologists say that the ideas that change history must have the quality of novelty and simplicity; this also has that of truth. And ideas assert themselves with a speed proportionate to their historical necessity. This is why we are "resigned" to winning... because, obviously, we cannot lose. This is, therefore, our prophetic utopia[17].

---

16 E. Pound, op. cit., p. 7, note 1.
17 Utopia in the scientific field does not exist. Whoever had said a century ago that he would go to the Moon would have been considered crazy. We realize that transforming people from debtors into owners of their currency is much more "utopian" than going to the Moon. After the discovery of induced value as a phenomenon pertaining to the science of law, the implementation of popular ownership of money is not only possible, but necessary to eliminate the seigniorage of large-scale usury.

Contributions on money

1) Notes on the philosophy of value

Space coincides only with the present, everything else is time. All schools of social and economic sciences have so far found themselves unable to carry out a serious scientific investigation because they lacked the presuppositions of the philosophy of value that are absolutely indispensable for knowing and defining the object itself of their research. Because every serious scientific procedure, free from the banal and gratuitous constructions of empirical pragmatism, starts from the clarification of an initial postulate whose truthfulness can only be ascertained and not demonstrated, we assume the postulate that value is a relationship between phases of time. So for example. the pen has value because it is expected to write, the knife has value because it is expected to cut, the coin has value because it is expected to buy, etc. So the value is the ratio between the moment of prediction and the foreseen moment. Given that time is the ego that presents itself as reality as an ongoing ability to remember, observe and predict, it might seem, at first glance, that there is no objective dimension of time because it coincides with the thinking ego. Instead, we realize that objective time exists as long as we take into account the fundamental hermeneutic principle of specifying the observation point of phenomenal reality. Since the constant of time is the present which is the thinking ego in its vital continuity, the observation point of reality is the present ego. The remembered moment and the foreseen moment are obviously not the present: they are thought and non-thinking times.

The objective reality of the present is space. In fact, space coincides only with the present. Everything else is time. The present ego of monetary time is the bearer of the coin which is the observation point that allows its objective spatial evaluation (which is the possession of the symbol) and temporal (which is the prediction of being able to buy). So, when monetarists claim to define value as a property of matter – e.g. the intrinsic value of gold as a property of the metal - they fall into the incurable mistake of considering the value in the dimension of space and since we have highlighted that the value is always a prediction, that is, a dimension of time, they fall into the absurd claim of going to the search for value where there is none.

Gold also has value by convention, that is, by predicting the acceptance of others as a condition of one's own acceptance, as a measure of value and the value of the measure. In fact, everyone is willing to accept money for goods because they expect to in turn give money for goods. Even in gold, traditionally used as a monetary symbol, the phenomenon of legal induction has occurred.

Gold, like any currency, even if it is made up of zero-cost symbols, is a legal entity because it has a merely conventional value. Having said this, it appears clear that the raw material for making money is the same that is used to make legal cases, *i.e.* spiritual form and reality, *i.e.* symbol and monetary convention.

Since the possible forms of law are: written, word, behavior (this is the case of commodity money whose value arises from the constant repetition of the conclusive behavior of acceptance), advertising and light (like the green and red of traffic lights are forms of a "having to be" legal, so computer lights have become "monetary symbols"), are also the possible forms of money. Only on these premises can the fundamental distinction between physiology and pathology of value be placed as a prerequisite for all scientific categories in which the researcher must have full awareness that his cognitive capacity is normal in the organic and contextual coordination of the temporal and spatial dimension.

The value judgment is normal only if the objective instrumental moment is distinguished from the subjective hedonic moment. This means that value judgment is normal only if it is based on a dualistic conception of philosophy of knowledge that distinguishes between subject and object. The instrumental moment is the objective moment of value because it is the objective moment of time. The hedonic moment is the subjective moment of value because it is the subjective moment of time. It always coincides with the present, that is, with the thinking ego. The value judgment is abnormal when the instrumental moment is confused with the hedonistic one, that is, when, in application of the monistic conception of the philosophy of knowledge which reduces reality to the idea of reality, the object is confused with the subject and therefore the instrumental moment, objective with the hedonistic, subjective one. The macroscopic consequence of this deformation of the value judgment is the phenomenon of the personification of the instrument which has determined in corporate law the shocking cultural disease of so called instrumental subjectivity whereby the company is not considered as the set of members linked by an organic relationship, but as a concept without human content: a true legal phantom.

The true and unspeakable purpose of the cultural strategy that conceived and created the phenomenon of instrumental subjectivity was to allow exploiting societies with the monstrous organic representation of the hedonistic moment of value, which is capitalism. Which is to say that while the people take on the function of being hungry, the government assuming that of eating on behalf of the people.

The historical experience of Hegelian rationalism has taught us that monism has been exploited to confuse the object with the subject, that is, the I with the non-I, that is, the I with You and mine with yours, so that yours can become mine. This is why Hegel is the philosopher of capitalism.

Having reduced the concept of society to an instrument, that is, to a concept without human content, the inevitable consequence was the replacement of the rule of serving oneself with that of serving (proper of organic society and natural law) because it is ridiculous to think that one can serve an instrument. Consequently, the natural ethics of being right has been replaced by economic ethics: what is right is right. The social interest here cannot coincide with that of the members because the "instrumental company" is not "the members". Thus, under the appearance of social interest, **a legal phantom is masked which is nothing more than the screen of the great mangers of exploiting societies**. This is why with the advent of instrumental subjectivities, **we have lived and are necessarily living only times of decadence because the worst are in charge.** In fact, once reality is reduced to the thinking Ego, no other utility is admitted than the utility of the Ego and consequently utility is reduced to selfishness.

On these premises we explain the phenomenon of tangentopoli which cannot be considered as an occasional statistical increase in political delinquency, but as a sign of the times. It is the historical projection of the great cultural disease of Hegelian monism.

The instruments used for the establishment of the monstrous organic representation of the hedonistic moment of value are essentially constitutional states (both liberal and socialist), central banks, joint-stock companies and multinationals. Since the enjoyment of goods is practically achieved in the right of property – which is precisely "legally protected enjoyment of goods" – capitalism has achieved the expropriation of peoples either with the constitutional norm of socialist states in state capitalism, or with money nominal (which is debt money because it is issued on loan by central banks) in the usurocratic capitalism of liberal states, or with the contribution of capital in joint-stock companies in which the member is transformed from owner into shareholder, i.e. creditor of an uncollectable loan equal to the entire contributed capital.

In all these cases, the common denominator is that ownership apparently becomes a legal phantom, essentially exploiting companies: the *nomenclature* in socialist states, *freemasonry* in liberal ones, the majority union of the shareholding package (which has nothing to do do with the majority of shareholders) in the so called joint-stock companies: essentially banks and multinationals.

On these premises we realize that the human community today lives in a system that has the prerogatives of livestock breeding and not those of human society. This was possible because a strategy of domination was achieved through an initiatory culture based on Hegelian principles of economic ethics. Only on these premises is it possible to explain why, simultaneously with the birth of nominal money, banks were all conceived as instrumental subjectivities. In fact, with the Bank of England (1694) the monstrous organic representation of the hedonistic moment of value was achieved, transforming people from owners into debtors of their own money because the rule of allowing the bank to issue money only by lending it was established and consolidated. And if we consider that the sum of the monetary units of measurement incorporates a value, i.e. a purchasing power equal to that of all real goods measured or measurable in value, this mirror-duplicated value can take on either the positive sign of property - and in this case the wealth of the people doubles - or the negative sign of the debt which plunges the people into the anguish of inevitable insolvency.

In fact, when the Central Bank issues money by lending it – as happens today – it charges the cost of money by 200% because it expropriates and indebts the community of its money, with the further increase in interest. It is no coincidence that **the transformation of peoples from owners into debtors of their own money (through the replacement of gold coins with nominal money) occurred at the same time as two instrumental subjectivities (based on the economistic ethics of serving oneself instead of serving): the constitutional state and the central bank.**

2) The Euro is an inconvenient currency. Why?

When the loan shark does something there is always a reason. Everyone has understood, through daily painful experience, that the euro is an inconvenient currency. Only a few have understood the real why. General public opinion believes that it is an ineluctable necessity linked to the replacement of the old with the new currency. It is a false belief because the numbers are, in this case, freely programmable. As usual, the most difficult things to observe are the obvious things, such as the moustache, which cannot be seen because they are under the nose. The bearer of the euro is like the bearer of the moustache. In fact, the inconvenience of the euro constitutes an incentive to use credit or debit cards which replace the *argent de poche,* i.e. the money from one's own pockets, with bank money. With ATMs our pocket is transformed into a real banking agency on which the costs for the related deposit and withdrawal services are calculated. The bank, in this way, makes use of our pockets as if it were the headquarters of its own agency, without paying rent and acquires control over further liquidity that would otherwise be unattainable.

The euro is like the number of the beast, which the Apocalypse speaks of, which is on the forehead and on the hand and which is used for buying and selling. It adds to the undue debt of current money the further damage of spontaneous slavery towards great usury.

3) The "colonial" currency

We have been saying this for years and the facts are proving us right: The euro is a second-class currency because it operates in an inorganic market; the European market, in fact, lacks energy sources. Only uneducated economists can consider the euro as a suitable currency for consolidating the prerogatives of sovereignty.

To make a comparison, today the euro is like a factory that can produce all but one of the basic necessities; **the euro can buy everything except oil, and when Europe needs oil it has to use the dollar.** History, a teacher of life, has taught that at a time when Europe was completing the organic nature of the market by opening up to Eastern markets, America intervened in Kosovo with the ridiculous pretext of fighting oil smuggling. This is why the euro cannot assume anything other than the function of colonial currency. More than five years have passed since we said that the dollar would disintegrate the euro for two reasons: because it had an interest in doing so, and because it has the strength to do so. The result of the monetary strategy, imposed on the European market by the leaders of the Federal Reserve Bank, was predicted by Giuseppe Palladino who defined it as stagflation, which means economic stagnation and monetary undervaluation, today improperly referred to as inflation, which occurs when the quantity of money in circulation is too abundant compared to the production increases.

Today money is scarce and undervalued, so there is a double push towards poverty, because money is scarce and worth little. The great usurers conceived t this way because they want to expropriate the people, putting them in debt of heir money, furthermore rarefying it with usurocratic banking techniques. Europe is under the sword of Damocles of the great usurer just like Argentina. The only response to this aggression of great usury is the popular ownership of he currency, that is, taking away the ownership of the currency from the Central Bank (a private company) and attributing it to the people at the time of ssuance.

4) The scandalous falsity of scandals or the true scandal of falsities?

With the discovery of induced value, not only does the reading of history change but also that of financial statements.

The dramatic explosion of gigantic scandals that affects the leaders of the major American economic complexes of global dimensions is, in our opinion, caused by the fact that all economic schools have not yet understood what money is. The macroscopic consequence of this cultural disease is: either the claim to deny the existence of money as an economic good (defining it, according to the theses of monetary nihilism, as "nothingness" or "neutral instrument of exchange"), or that of proposing the definition as "debit and/or credit". If the first hypothesis were true, it should be indifferent to us whether we have money in our pockets or not and the money thieves should be set free because they would have stolen "nothing". If the second were true, a debt of money would be "a debt of a debt". While the first hypothesis was taken into consideration only by the economists of literary salons, the second is the one which, unfortunately, was taken into consideration by the drafters of the balance sheets of central banks and multinationals because they were forced to admit, albeit incorrectly, that money exists. An old farmer, a friend of mine, taught me that the worst defect of the louse is not that it sucks blood, but that it is an idiot because it doesn't know how to do anything else: and the idiot is more dangerous than the criminal because it is totally unpredictable.

Once it has been demonstrated that money is a real good because it is not only a measure of value, but also the value of measurement (because each unit of measurement necessarily has the quality corresponding to what it must measure: just as the meter has the quality of length because it measures length, money has the quality of value because it measures value) the entire American economic system is in deficit because the distinction between induced value and credit value is missing, *i.e.* between money and debt, all balance sheets inevitably also report the value of money to debt as it is conceived as debt money which is the so called nominal currency or, to put it in Ciampi's words (draft law proposed by the Ciampi Government on 10 February 1993) "bad debt" (as if to say "dry water").

The American crisis could be caused by a macroscopic falsification of financial statements in which monetary values are reported as debit, *i.e.* as negative values, which are instead highly positive asset values because of zero cost (since they are produced, like every unit of measurement, by the simple mental activity of the social convention), consolidated in the purchasing power which mirror-image duplicates the value of all real goods measured or measurable in value. In this way, the debt currency, instead of speculatively duplicating the value of real assets, *i.e.* the wealth of the American people, plunges them into the anguish of inevitable insolvency because, at the time of issuance, the cost of money is 200%, as it transforms "+ 100%" into "- 100%". Cultural diseases are the most harmful. As you can see, my farmer friend was right: idiots (monetarists) are more dangerous than criminals, and the principle applies not only to America, but has a global dimension. **My advice to the President of the USA is, therefore, to have the budgets reviewed taking into account the distinction between money and debt (that is, debt and the means to pay it).** Even the Bank of Italy has always reported the currency it issued by lending as debt in its balance sheets. **Lending is a quality of the owner, not of the debtor.** You can fool part of the world part of the time or all the world part of the time or part of the world all the time, but you can't fool all the world all the time.

5) The reason for the "wall against wall" between *Confindustria* and the trade unions. The diseases of surplus value and flexibility

In social bodies, wrong ideas are like diseases of the human body: and there are two chronic diseases in the world of work: surplus value and flexibility. When Marx stated that the employer parasitically exploited the worker because he appropriated the profit margin, *i.e.* the surplus value, he laid the ideological premise on which the union was born as an instrument of revolution with the aim of claiming, in the form of an increase in wages, the surplus value. Since free labor is distinguished from slave labor because it is based on the free negotiation of compensation, the exaggerated application of the theory of surplus value destroys the labor contract because it destroys the employer's interest in contracting. This cultural disease is the precursor to either

24

unemployment or work without a contract (which is the return to slavery or at least to illegal work).

With the advent of globalization and international competition in labor markets, this disease has become so aggravated that it has exploded into conflict not only between employers and unions, but also with government authorities. The prognosis has become decidedly poor with the second disease of flexibility, the treatment of which is impossible because the diagnosis was wrong. With flexibility, the reduction in the purchasing power of wages is not attributable to the employer or the government, but to the heads of the central banks because only these have the power to arbitrarily determine deflationary pressures or monetary undervaluation by forcing entrepreneurs to either cease productive activities, or to accept flexibility by adapting costs and prices to the fluctuations in monetary values that drive the globalization of markets itself. **Therefore the trade union demands with the related protests** (including the so-called intangibility of art. 18 of the workers statute) **should not be raised as trade union conflicts towards the employers, but towards the Central Bank, in a united manner by the government, employers and workers.**

Flexibility in fact concerns the purchasing power of the currency. Induced value has nothing to do with surplus value. The radical solution to these problems (and not only these) lies in the implementation of the principle of popular ownership of money. Only by returning the currency to its legitimate owners will it be possible to rationalize the system. It is no coincidence that St. Thomas states that ethics is an aspect of rationality.

6) The "trap" of the art. 130 of the Treaty. Europe like Argentina?

Yes! The validity of this diagnosis is based on two fundamental arguments:

A) the art. 130 of the Treaty:

Article 130

When exercising the powers and carrying out the tasks and duties conferred upon them by the Treaties and the Statute of the ESCB and of the ECB, neither the European Central Bank, nor a national central bank, nor any member of their decision-making bodies shall seek or take instructions from Union institutions, bodies, offices or agencies, from any government of a Member State or from any other body. The Union institutions, bodies, offices or agencies

25

and the governments of the Member States undertake to respect this principle and not to seek to influence the members of the decision-making bodies of the European Central Bank or of the national central banks in the performance of their tasks.

B) the advent of the euro.

At the first reading of the Treaty, although unpleasantly surprised by Article 130, we did not understand the real reason why. Today, after the drama in Argentina, we finally understood it. The art. 130 – which prohibits any possibility of contact or interference between the Member States and the European Central Bank in the issuance phase – was officially justified on the principle of the need to safeguard the euro from inflationary pressures or stresses. (This need could have been satisfied on the basis of the normal criteria of "technical discretion" well known to the schools of banking statistics, so much so that this rule has no precedent.)

The truth is that they wanted to raise an insurmountable wall similar to the one that separates states from foreign central banks. **In other words, with art. 130 the relationship between European States and the ECB is identical to that existing between Argentina and the American Federal Reserve Bank.** On these premises, the issuance of the euro is made by the ECB as if it were **a loan to a foreign state.** Apparently, since central banks only issue money by lending it, it might seem that there is no difference between issuing money domestically or abroad, while we know very well – and the drafters of the aforementioned 130 know it better than us – that **the loan abroad is drastically required to be repaid by international law and custom, as it is made in favor of strangers;** the internal loan is attenuated and/or deferred due to the contacts and solicitations that normally characterize the relationships between the central bank and the government: **those same contracts that the high banking lodge has carefully wanted to avoid as they are particularly annoying to the regime's usurers.** In other words, with art. 130 and the advent of the euro, Europe is in the same subordination that Argentina has towards the dollar. In fact, it goes into debt for debts that are not due to the ECB, for a value equal to the entire euro in circulation, without any possibility of being able to prevent the sword of Damocles of debts (which are not due), from falling , as in Argentina, on his head. The very fact that the art. 130 was promptly inserted into the Maastricht Treaty, in unsuspecting times, makes us think that the "Damocles *pro tempore*", governor Duisenberg, has serious intentions of throwing the sword, copying what his colleague, Alan Greespan, did with

Argentina. Therefore the "sword" exists and is over our heads. We hope it doesn't fall, but this hope is not enough. **This is why it is necessary to prepare an emergency currency that allows us to fill monetary gaps similar to the Argentine ones.** Money is like blood, its quantity must be adequate for the size of the body to be supplied, and its availability for transfusion must be arranged, eliminating the risk of fatal collapse. The Argentine Government understood this truth and designed the alternative currency, the Argentine, whose issuance was prevented, as is known, by the intervention of supranational usurocratic authorities. Our advantage is given by the fact that – on the initiative of the SAUS Anti-Usury Union – the alternative currency, the SIMEC, has already been created in Italy, which allows us to deal with times of emergency because it is designed in such a way that it cannot be controlled by the central banking system as it was born "owned by the bearer" and "without reserve", like gold, and obtained the chrism of legitimacy with the Order of the Court of Chieti (of 21 September 2000, n. 127) and the publication in the Euro-Catalogue unified version of the Italian currency (Alfa Edizioni, Turin, 2001, page 791, where it is officially listed: "Current virtual value: 1000 Simec = 2000 lire"). It is therefore necessary to promote the euro-simec and/or simec-euro conversion through convertibility funds established for this purpose, giving the fund not the ownership, but only the availability for the exchange. In this way the transferor, owner of the fund, remains the owner of both the euros and the SIMECs to which he is entitled.

7) The first to denounce the gigantic scam was Carlo Marx. "Reduce taxes by eliminating waste"???!!!

Waste must be eliminated as such and not to "reduce taxes". On this essential premise, we enthusiastically accept President Berlusconi's program. Therefore, in the fundamental rule that before considering the straw it is best to deal with the beam, it must be said that **the greatest and fundamental "fiscal waste" is the payment to the central bank of the debt not owed for all the money in circulation.** The citizen thinks, in good faith, that the tax levy is intended for the payment of expenses necessary for public utility purposes. Nothing could be further from the truth. As is known and irrefutable, most of the withdrawals end up in the pockets of the Central Bank's shareholders (a S.p.A., a private for-profit company) because the central bank only issues money by lending it. And since lending money is the owner's prerogative, and the owner must be the one who creates the value of the money – that is, the one who accepts it and not the one who prints it – the fee due to the central bank must be commensurate with that normally due to a printing house. Therefore here **the "fiscal waste" is equal to the difference between printing cost and nominal value of the**

currency. It could have had a semblance of reliability to finalize the tax levy towards the payment of debts to the central bank, when the monetary issue was based on the reserve. Since lending money is the owner's prerogative, the bank could say: "the money is mine because the reserve is mine, therefore I can issue the money by lending it". With the end of the Bretton Woods agreements, on 15 August 1971 there was historical as well as scientific proof of the uselessness of the reserve, otherwise the dollar, from that date, would have had to totally lose its value because it was deprived of the reserve. **Therefore, the value of the currency is created by the community that accepts it and not the bank that issues it.** Upon issuance, two different legal instruments are conventionally created: the loan and the object of the loan: the debt and the object of the debt. When the tax withdrawal is made to pay this debt, the taxpayer pays to return his money to the bank which instead should be credited to him because it is he himself who, by accepting it, creates its value. On these premises, the ridiculous definitions given by monetarists connected to the system are explained such as: "money is nothing"[18] or "bad debt"[19] with the evident aim of concealing the object of **the scam with which the peoples were transformed from owners (when the currency was gold) into debtors of their own currency** (with the nominal currency).

The first to masterfully denounce this gigantic scam was Carl Marx: «*Since their birth the large banks, adorned with national names, have been nothing more than companies of speculators who worked alongside governments and, thanks to the privileges obtained, were able to anticipate* (i.e. "lend", editor's note) *them money. Therefore the accumulation of public debt* (paid with tax levies, editor's note) *is no more infallible measure than the progressive rise of the shares of these banks, whose development dates back to the foundation of the Bank of England* (1694). *The Bank of England began by lending its money to the government at eight per cent, at the same time it was authorized by Parliament to mint money with the same capital and returned to lend it again to the public in the form of banknotes. It did not take long for this credit currency, manufactured by the Bank of England itself, to become the currency with which the bank itself made loans to the State and paid the interest on the public debt on behalf of the State. However, it was not enough for the Bank to give with one hand to have more returned with the other, but, even as it received, it remained a perpetual creditor towards the Nation, up to the last cent it had given.* »[20]

---

18 Massimo Fini, The devil's dung coin, Marsilio, Venice.
19 Bill proposed by the Ciampi Government on 10 February 1993, in Parliamentary Acts.
20 C. Marx, Capital, book I, chapter. 24, par. 6, Edizioni Riunite, Rome 1974, pp. 817-818.

This message of Marx was totally ignored by all governments, even by so called Marxists. If the Berlusconi government does what it has declared it wants to do, eliminating the debt caused by the monetary issue scam, it will write a new page in history. In fact, there is no greater "waste" than the tax paid not only for a debt not owed, but even for one's own credit passed off as debt. That's why everyone can lend money except the issuer. Banking charity is stronger than Christian charity: Christian charity teaches how to remit debts, banking charity has even taught how to pay debtors: the central banks who collect their debt as creditors.

If President Berlusconi does not take this message of ours into account, he will prove that it is his intention to eliminate the waste of straws and not that of the beam.

8) Monetary strategies in the *F.I.A.T.* crisis

Umberto Agnelli, regarding the "F.I.A.T." crisis, spoke of the participation of a "strategic share". Strategic choices have the essential quality of being simple. Strategy is a science in which children's logic applies. To understand the real reason for the Turin crisis, it must first be highlighted that "F.I.A.T." is in crisis due to lack of money. Debt insolvency is in fact caused by the inability to pay them. At first glance this might seem like a joke. But no: This is the real crux of the problem. When the currency was gold, the rarity of the coin was rigid and uncontrollable because it was based on the "physical law" of the existence and availability of the metal. With the advent of nominal money and the abolition of the "gold reserve", rarity is arbitrarily programmed with the ferocious parsimony of the great usurers behind the counters of central banks.

FIAT never had liquidity problems when it controlled the syndicate of the majority of the share package of the shareholders (so-called "participants") of the Bank of Italy. With the advent of the Euro it became a drop in the bucket for ECB shareholders. And since, with globalization, the proverb "the whole world is a country" has historically occurred, because the world has become such, the conglomerate of central banks has been substantially unified in the same hands of the true masters, according to the masterly and prophetic definition by Marx: «*Since their birth, the large banks, adorned with national names, have been nothing more than companies of private speculators who worked alongside governments and, thanks to the privileges obtained, were able to lend them money.»*[21] This means that the distinction between central banks should not be deduced from the "national denominations" but from those of the "speculators" who control them. The "S.p.A.", instrumental subjectivities in which the central banks are constituted, are the screens of the great mangers because they allow the great usurers to steal secretly in anonymity (hence the exact qualification of "anonymous companies") transforming the people from owners into debtors of their money. On these premises it is explained why **the FIAT crisis was the consequence of the Argentine crisis where important Italian banks were bled to death by decision of the Federal Reserve Bank** which requested payment of undue debts incurred when the dollars were issued. **All the peoples of the world are subjected to the swords of the "Damocles *pro tempore*" masters of the central banks.** Europe is also in the same condition. It therefore seems appropriate to close this brief note with the words remembered by Ezra Pound: *«Saying that a state cannot pursue its goals for lack of money is like saying that an engineer cannot build roads for lack of kilometres.»*

9) The "Descent of the Barbarians"

When the barbarian hordes moved in medieval Europe they used spears, clubs, arrows, fire, stones. With the French Revolution the barbaric hordes of the great usurers, led by the Bank of England (defined by Ezra Pound as "liberal usurers"), replaced traditional weapons with the slogans of ideologies. The basic formula of all popular protests, *"Liberté, egalité, fraternité"*, was invented, they say, by an English banker. From then until today nothing has changed.

A few days ago the slogan "right to land" was launched on television, shouted by a crowd of non-EU citizens. **If we consider that the Kurds, a landless people, were transported to Italy at a cost of ten million each (equal to approximately 2582.28 euros) paid by the masters of the central banks, traditionally transporters of human herds such as slavers**, we realize that this slogan is the weapon conceived by them, **to establish between the Kurdish and Italian people the same relationship of incompatibility that exists between Palestinians and Israelis**. The barbaric hordes of usurers have invaded the world using the perfidious and refined weapons of slogans as strategies of domination based on aberrant psychological stimuli. In fact, **much more harmful than the blow of the sword is the guilt complex caused by the accusation of "racism" contested with the deafening clamor of the mass**

---

21   C. Marx, op. cit., pp. 817-818.

media against those who want to oppose the invasion of the human herds of non-EU citizens. The right to land is a sacrosanct right, provided that it is freed from the seigniorage of great usury. In fact, every people must be recognized as masters of their land on the condition that they are also masters, and not debtors, of their money at home.

Money to men is like water to fish. In times of drought, fish abandon the arid areas and go to puddles of water. Following this rule, the bankers of the 19th century, called the century of usury by Pound, moved millions of men from Europe to America, creating monetary rarity in Europe and an abundance of money in America. The big usurers have applied the same rule to the human herds of non-EU citizens. This is why, out of absolute imperative historical necessity, it is necessary to make every people the owner of its own currency.

The interest in returning to his land, to have his money, will arise spontaneously for every non-EU citizen, using the "law of water and fish", in the opposite direction to that of the usurer. Making every people the owner of its own currency is much more than a slogan: it is a powerful idea capable of writing new pages of history. **Moving from the era of usury** (born in 1694 with the debt currency of the Bank of England) **to that of civilization. This is the charismatic mission of our generation.**

10) The chain of Saint Anthony and the sword of Damocles that hangs from the hands of the great usurers

It is characteristic of the human soul to anticipate the expected values to the current moment. This is why the mercantile practice of using the bill of exchange not only as a promise to pay, but also as a means of payment, was born. With the bill of exchange, the provision of performance is strengthened by "legal certainty" as the debtor can be forced to pay by law. If the debtor pays the bill regularly, all the obligatory relationships established between endorsers and endorsers are satisfied. If it is not paid, the insolvency inexorably rebounds on all connected parties such as endorsers and endorsers in the circulation of the bill of exchange. This is how the scam of the so called Saint Anthony chain letter was born and explains why the bill protest contested against the insolvent debtor is considered by the legislator with particular severity as it undermines the trust in monetary circulation. **The most serious form of chain letter is monetary issuance.** The nominal currency was in fact born as a bill of exchange issued by the governor of the central bank (e.g. with the formula "One thousand lire payable on sight to the bearer" signed: The Governor of the Bank of Italy), not in the capacity of "citizen" but of "iron recommended". In fact, while if the citizen does not pay he is liable for insolvency with the loss of legal dignity in the capacity of "protested bill of exchange", the governor not only issues the bill with the guarantee of not paying it, but – while signing it as a debtor – issues it by lending it, that is, as a creditor. The object of this loan would therefore be an uncollectible debt of the banker who is, therefore, a true creditor and false debtor of real money passed off as a false bill of exchange.

When the monetary issue was based on the reserve, the currency could be considered as a bill of exchange, as it was conceived as a credit instrument representing the reserve. The banker could well have said: *"the money is mine because the reserve is mine"*. Once the reserve has been abolished, with the end of the Bretton Woods agreements, we finally have historical proof that the monetary value is purely conventional, like that of an antique stamp. Money has value simply because we agree that it has value. Therefore the money must belong to those who accept it and not to those who issue it: it must belong to the people and not to the bank. By paying what is due, at the time of the issue the banker has hung the sword of Damocles on the St. Anthony's chain because he is in the position either to lend each people their own currency and renew the loan by profiting not only from the money but also from the interest, or to make the sword of Damocles fall by demanding the payment of debts not owed, as the Federal Reserve Bank did with Argentina. **If we do not take back ownership of our money, the whole world will continue to live under the sword of Damocles hanging from the chain of St. Anthony which hangs from the hands of the giants of the large-scale usury underworld.**

11) Money like blood

Just as blood distributes oxygen throughout the body, money distributes purchasing power to the market. This elementary principle was not understood by the asinineries of monetarists because, while the object taken and transported by the red blood cell is known exactly as "oxygen", the definition of monetary oxygen was missing until today: the induced value which is the power of purchase, *i.e.* the expectation of being able to purchase given to the bearer of the money as a pure conventional value. This fundamental and very serious cultural gap is based on an even more serious ignorance of the concept of value itself. Value is always a prediction, that is, a dimension of time and not of space; it is a spiritual reality and not a commodity.

The coin, despite having a zero cost symbol, has value because it gives the bearer the expectation of being able to buy. The category of monetary values has thus constituted the cultural monopoly of the initiatory school of the great usurers of the central banks, while the teaching of the two hypotheses has been reserved for the "human cattle":
a) monetary nihilism (for which money is nothing and only the real goods being exchanged would have value);
b) the bearer's debt currency, c. d. nominal money (which the bank owns and, as such, issues by lending it).

The common denominator of these two choices is the threat of death of the market; in the first case by asphyxiation because the very existence of monetary oxygen is denied; in the second case by poisoning since the bearer is conceived not as the owner, but as the debtor of his coin. About these aberrant theories dominates the hegemony of the usurer who can easily rob the people after having convinced them either that the object of the theft is nothingness, or that he must accept his own currency at the time of issue with the equivalent of the debt not owed, *i.e.* on loan. On these premises we understand the difference not only between nominal money – the bearer's debt and gold coin – the bearer's property, but also between two different conceptions of life, between the British Commonwealth and the Holy Roman Empire, between barbarism and civilization, between ethics economics of instrumental subjectivity for which the social function operates on the rule of serving (it is no coincidence that all the banks in the world are legal ghosts – LLCs) and natural ethics of organic society (made up of living men) based on the rule of serving. Only after having clarified that monetary oxygen is purchasing power (*i.e.* the value of money created by social convention) just as in the blood system the blood cells also carry oxygen into the capillary vessels, so money must be distributed recognizing everyone's right to his share of citizen's income, as the owner and not as a debtor of his currency.

Citizens' pockets are the capillaries of the monetary system. Heretical economists rightly remind us that the best place to keep money is in people's pants[22].

We are breathing the poisoned air of debt money issued since 1694, following the example of the Bank of England, by all the banks in the world. **With the advent of the globalization of markets, we can already feel the first signs of monetary wars which are the precursor to deadly ones.** This is why there is

---

22 «The safest place of storage is in the pants of the people», in E. Pound, op. cit., p. 72.

a need to prevent them with a global reform for true and definitive monetary justice.

Every currency – regardless of the state or central bank that issues it – must be declared, by international convention, the property of the bearer and without reserve. The only currency accepted, up to now, conventionally by all states in the world has been gold. If you want to establish a new universal currency, you have to copy gold. To date this has not been possible because the cultural basis to do so was lacking.

This currency, conceived (like the SIMEC) on the new discovery of induced value, must have the positive qualities of gold: bearer properties without reserve and not the negative ones of the high production cost and exaggerated and uncontrollable rarity.

Since the price is not only the index of the value of the goods, but also of the saturation point of the market, the market should be considered saturated, both with goods and with money, only when prices tend to coincide with production costs. This is the true law of monetary rarity which must be institutionalized in an international convention to free people from arbitrary rarefactions of money and real goods. If money is the blood of the market, there must be neither too much nor too little money, otherwise there would be, due to monetary imbalances, the analogous diseases of anemia or hyperemia.

Since the monetary function is a constitutive, essential element of political sovereignty, the following anecdote deserves to be remembered. When Machiavelli was asked what the most important quality of the prince was, he replied: *"The sense of proportion"*. This is why the usurer cannot be a prince. The sense of measure is incompatible with the ferocious parsimony on which the central bank and the debt currency have been programmed; the so called nominal money that transformed people from owners into debtors of monetary values.

We have been patient for 329 years. Now stop! The revenge of blood against the gold of usurocracy is the new page of history for the new generations.

A radical and definitive monetary restoration is required to finally return to breathing clean monetary oxygen, purified from the poison of debt not due to the seigniorage of great usury.

2) Is the Euro as strong as the "Quota 90" lira?

Alberto De Stefani – who was Minister of the Treasury and Finance of the first fascist government and professor of Economics and Financial Science in the Faculty of Political Sciences at the "La Sapienza" University of Rome – told me: «Mussolini lost the war with "quota 90".» I thus learned that the "quote 90" was the operation with which the lira was revalued compared to the pound by 25%: the price of the pound was reduced from 120 to 90 lire.

Mussolini accepted the project with enthusiasm because the consultants of the Bank of Italy (Stringer, Paratore, Beneduce and Volpi di Misurata) proposed it as a signal of prestige and strengthening of the dignity of the Italian State at an international level. "Stronger lira" meant, for Mussolini, "stronger Italy", exactly as today, for Duisenberg and Prodi, "stronger euro" means "stronger Europe".

De Stefani made me understand that, with the monetary reevaluation of 25%, credits and debts increased by the same percentage. The banks became rich and the companies went bankrupt due to the unjustified and unpredictable increase in debts contracted to finance production activities.

Italy entered the war unarmed due to the failures caused by the inevitable insolvency following the unjustified increase in the value of the money subject to the debt. Nothing new under the sun. With the revaluation of the euro, everyone praised the strong currency, exactly as Mussolini did with the "90 quota". On this basis we can understand why America has closed the importation of steel from Europe. Since the price of steel largely offset the payment for oil, Europe today finds itself not only unable to pay for oil, but also with a further increase in its debt due to the blockade of exports and of the revaluation of the euro.

There is only one way to free ourselves from the slavery of great usury: popular ownership of money. Making every people the master of their currency at the time of issuance means taking away the hegemony of seigniorage from the central banks, **in a regime of integral democracy in which every people has not only political sovereignty, but also monetary sovereignty.** *Carthago delenda est.*

13) Bill for popular ownership of the Euro

HONORABLE PARLIAMENTARY MEMBERS!

The aim of this proposal is to fill a legislative gap that is no longer tolerable, already reported, moreover, by the bill "Popular ownership of money" (Senate XII Legislature, n. 1282, communicated to the Presidency on 11 January 1995) on the initiative of Senator Natali and others and, subsequently (Senate XIII Legislature, n. 1288), on the initiative of Senator Monteleone and others. In fact, no rule establishes who should own the Euro at the original moment of its acceptance. The truth is that money has value because, being a measure of value, it is also, necessarily, a value of measure. In fact, each unit of measurement has the quality corresponding to what it must measure: just as the meter has the quality of length because it measures length, the coin has the quality of value because it measures value. Therefore the monetary symbol is not only the formal manifestation of the monetary convention, but also the container of the value induced and incorporated into the symbol which is precisely the value of the measure or purchasing power. With the discovery of induced value as pure legal value (see G. Auriti, *L'ordinamento internazionale del sistema monetario*, Edigrafital, Teramo 1993, p. 43 *et seq.*) the scientific justification of monetary value was finally given. As has been demonstrated, a case similar to that of physical induction occurs here. Just as mechanical energy is transformed into electrical energy in the dynamo, so in money the value of the convention is transformed, that is, of a legal instrument into a real good object of property rights: **money**. In short, the value of the currency is caused not by the activity of the issuing body – which, by preparing and dispensing the symbols, determines only the formal presupposition of the monetary value – but by its acceptance by the community. The issuing of symbols in accordance with legal tender (the so-called forced tender) is an act of "heteronomy", the acceptance of the currency, which conventionally determines its value, is an act of "autonomy". The value of the Euro is born and persists in its continuity because it is conventionally accepted as a measure of the value and value of the measure being exchanged. For these reasons the Euro is and cannot be anything other than the property of the bearer who, with his conclusive behavior, contributes to causing and maintaining its value. The Maastricht Treaty rightly limits itself to considering the first phase of the issue, it completely ignores the creative moment of the monetary value, so much so that no provision of the treaty considers who has the right of ownership over the Euro and how it should be attributed . The content of the paper declaration affixed to the symbol by the issuing body is particularly significant. In it only the word "Euro" appears preceded by the numerical expression and the signature of the Governor under the acronym, in various languages, of the European Central Bank with the year of issue. From this point of view, the clear difference is clear with the currencies of the Member States which traditionally conceived the currency as a credit instrument representing the reserve. The central bank was, in fact, considered the owner of the value of the currency because it was considered the owner of the value of the reserve, as such legitimated to issue money by lending it because lending is the owner's prerogative. Once the monetary reserve was abolished with the end of the Bretton Woods Agreements (15 August 1971), we had the replacement of the conventional value to the credit one. This explains the "silence" as the "object" of the paper declaration of the Euro since the issue can no longer be justified by loan because it lacks the (otherwise absurd) justification of the reserve, **reliance is placed on the mere consolidated practice in parasitic, traditional seigniorage of central banks.** In fact, once it has been demonstrated that the value of the currency is created not by those who issue it, but by those who accept it, lending money upon issuance means imposing a cost of money of 200%. When the two phases of issuance and acceptance are made to coincide, a serious injustice results in the legal regime of monetary values. This historically occurred with the advent of nominal money and the central banking system. Once upon a time, whoever found a gold nugget appropriated it without incurring debt to the mine. Today, in place of the mine there is the central bank, in place of the nugget a piece of paper, in place of property there is debt because the bank only issues money by lending it, while those who create its value are those who accept it. The merely instrumental moment of the emission of symbols has invaded the hedonistic moment of the ownership of money, so that **the central bank, by issuing money by lending it, expropriates and indebts the community of its own money without compensation.** That's why everyone can lend money except the issuer. By leveraging the conditioned reflex caused by the age-old habit of always giving a consideration for having money, the central banks, confusing the issuance phase with that of circulation, have induced all the peoples of the world to accept their own currency, upon of the issue, with the consideration for the debt, *i.e.* on loan. With the replacement of gold coins with nominal money, people were thus transformed from owners into debtors of their own money in the greatest scam of all time, which went unnoticed because it was too obvious. This originated in 1694 with the issuing of the pound and the establishment of the Bank of England. Today, with the advent of the Euro, Europe finds itself in the privileged position of being able to replace the debt currency owned by the central bank with its own currency. In fact, no provision of the Maastricht Treaty considers who should own the Euro. This is proof that the treaty only considers the issuing phase and ignores the acceptance phase. (Probably this happened because we relied on the possibility of continuing the monstrous practice of "usurocratic seigniorage", whereby the European peoples would have to go into debt, without compensation towards the ECB for a value equal to the entire Euro in circulation.) This means that it is left to the exclusive competence of the European Peoples to autonomously regulate the regime of acceptance and ownership of the currency on which the ECB has no power to interfere similarly to the preclusion of member states from interfering in the issuing phase pursuant to the art. 130 of the Maastricht Treaty. Since "*qui tacet neque adfirmat neque negat*", it appears clear that the European Central Bank, due to the limit imposed by the essential and univocal meaning of the word "acceptance" as the exclusive competence of those who accept, and not of those who issue, can do nothing other than take note of the principle that **the ownership of the Euro arises from the explicit recognition of uniform conventional law, as the property of the European Peoples for the sole fact that, by accepting it, they create its value.** The acceptance of the Euro as the property of the bearer allows the achievement of two further objectives of fundamental importance: 1) using the currency as an instrument of social law in implementation of the 2nd paragraph. of the art. 42 of the Constitution which establishes access to property for all, creating a personal right with patrimonial content, such as citizenship income; 2) **rationalize the tax system by allowing the State to retain at source what is necessary for the needs of public utility, eliminating costs and times of purely accounting and unproductive work and the risks of tax evasion.** Given the imminence of the circulation of the Euro, we ask that this bill be questioned under an emergency procedure.

BILL

Art. 1 - The Euro, upon acceptance, becomes the property of the citizens and is acquired, for this purpose, at the disposal of the Member States adhering to the Maastricht Treaty. The Euro is therefore the property of the bearer.

Art. 2 - Each citizen is assigned a social income code, through which he is credited with the share of income caused by monetary acceptance and other possible sources of income in implementation of the 2nd paragraph. of the art. 42 of the Constitution.

Art. 3 – While the ownership of the Euro is accepted in representation of the national collectivity, the Government is entitled to withhold at origin what is necessary for the fiscal needs of public utility.

Art. 4 - Transitional rule. A debt moratorium is granted upon request by a party, pending verification of who owns the Euro at the time of issue.

John Fitzgerald Kennedy

35th President of the United States: 1961 - 1963

Executive Order 11110—Amendment of Executive Order No. 10289 as Amended, Relating to the Performance of Certain Functions Affecting the Department of the Treasury
June 04, 1963

By virtue of the authority vested in me by section 301 of title 3 of the United States Code, it is ordered as follows:

SECTION 1. Executive Order No. 10289 of September 19, 1951, as amended, is hereby further amended --

(a) By adding at the end of paragraph 1 thereof the following subparagraph (j):

"(j) The authority vested in the President by paragraph (b) of section 43 of the Act of May 12, 1933, as amended (31 U.S.C. 821 (b)), to issue silver certificates against any silver bullion, silver, or standard silver dollars in the Treasury not then held for redemption of any outstanding silver certificates, to prescribe the denominations of such silver certificates, and to coin standard silver dollars and subsidiary silver currency for their redemption," and

(b) By revoking subparagraphs (b) and (c) of paragraph 2 thereof.

SEC. 2. The amendment made by this Order shall not affect any act done, or any right accruing or accrued or any suit or proceeding had or commenced in any civil or criminal cause prior to the date of this Order but all such liabilities shall continue and may be enforced as if said amendments had not been made.

JOHN F. KENNEDY

THE WHITE HOUSE,

June 4, 1963

Debt-Free United States Notes Were Once Issued Under JFK and the U.S. Government Still Has The Power to Issue Debt-Free Money

By *Michael T. Snyder*   Market Overview Dec 19, 2011 05:43AM ET

Most Americans have no idea that the U.S. government once issued debt-free money directly into circulation. America once thrived under a debt-free monetary system, and we can do it again. The truth is that the United States is a sovereign nation and it does not need to borrow money from anyone. Back in the days of JFK, Federal Reserve Notes were not the only currency in circulation. Under JFK (at at various other times), a limited number of debt-free United States Notes were issued by the U.S. Treasury and spent by the U.S. government without any new debt being created. In fact, each bill said "United States Note" right at the top. Unfortunately, United States Notes are not being issued today. If you stop right now and pull a dollar out of your wallet, what does it say right at the top? It says "Federal Reserve Note". Normally, the way our current system works is that whenever more Federal Reserve Notes are created more debt is also created. This debt-based monetary system is systematically destroying the wealth of this nation. But it does not have to be this way. The truth is that the U.S. government still has the power under the U.S. Constitution to issue debt-free money, and we need to educate the American people about this.

Posted below are pictures of the front and the back of a United States Note printed in 1963 while JFK was president....

Notice that there is a red seal instead of a green seal on the front, and it says "United States Note" rather than "Federal Reserve Note".

According to Wikipedia, United States Notes were issued

directly into circulation by the U.S. Treasury and they were first used during the Civil War....

"They were originally issued directly into circulation by the U.S. Treasury to pay expenses incurred by the Union during the American Civil War. Over the next century, the legislation governing these notes was modified many times and numerous versions have been issued by the Treasury."

So why are we using debt-based Federal Reserve Notes today instead of debt-free United States Notes?

It seems rather stupid, doesn't it?

Well, that is what Thomas Edison thought too.

Thomas Edison was once quoted in the New York Times as saying the following....

"That is to say, under the old way any time we wish to add to the national wealth we are compelled to add to the national debt.

Now, that is what Henry Ford wants to prevent. He thinks it is stupid, and so do I, that for the loan of $30,000,000 of their own money the people of the United States should be compelled to pay $66,000,000 — that is what it amounts to, with interest. People who will not turn a shovelful of dirt nor contribute a pound of material will collect more money from the United States than will the people who supply the material and do the work. That is the terrible thing about interest. In all our great bond issues the interest is always greater than the principal. All of the great public works cost *more than twice the actual cost, on that account. Under the present system of doing business we simply add 120 to 150 per cent, to the stated cost.*

But here is the point: If our nation can issue a dollar bond, it can issue a dollar bill. The element that makes the bond good makes the bill good."

Our current debt-based monetary system was devised by greedy bankers that wanted to make huge profits by creating money out of thin air and lending it to the U.S. government at interest.

Sadly, the vast majority of the American people have no idea how money is actually created in this nation.

In a previous article about money and debt, I explained how more government debt is created whenever the U.S. government puts more money into circulation....

"When the government wants more money, the U.S. government swaps U.S. Treasury bonds for "Federal Reserve notes", thus creating more government debt. Usually the money isn't even printed up - most of the time it is just electronically credited to the government. The Federal Reserve creates these "Federal Reserve notes" out of thin air. These Federal Reserve notes are backed by nothing and have no intrinsic value of their own."

When each new Federal Reserve Note is created, the interest owed by the federal government on that new Federal Reserve Note is not also created at the same time.

So the amount of government debt that is created actually exceeds the amount of money that is created.

Isn't that a stupid system?

The U.S. Constitution says that the federal government is the one that should actually be issuing our money.

In particular, according to Article I, Section 8 of the U.S. Constitution, it is the U.S. Congress that has been given the responsibility to "coin Money, regulate the Value thereof, and of foreign Coin, and fix the Standard of Weights and Measures".

So why is a private central banking cartel issuing our money?

As is the case with so many other issues, we desperately need to get back to the way the U.S. Constitution says that we should be doing things.

The debt-based Federal Reserve system is literally stealing the future from our children and our grandchildren.

Back in 1910, a couple years prior to the passage of the Federal Reserve Act, the national debt was only about $2.6 billion.

A little over 100 years later, our national debt is now more than 5000 times larger.

So why don't we just admit that this system simply does not work?

Our current debt-based monetary system also requires very high personal income taxes to pay for it.

In fact, it is no accident that the personal income tax was introduced at about the same time that the Federal Reserve system originally came into existence.

Our children, our grandchildren and many generations after that are facing a lifetime of debt slavery because of us.

As I have written about previously, if the federal government began right at this moment to repay the U.S. national debt at a rate of one dollar per second, it would take over 440,000 years to pay off the national debt.

Neither the Republicans or the Democrats are proposing any solutions to this problem. Rather, both parties are only trying to slow down the rate at which we are going into even more debt.

But the truth is that the federal government does not have to go into a single penny of additional debt.

How could this be?

It is not too complicated.

If Congress took back the power over our currency and started issuing debt-free money a lot of our problems could be fixed.

A basic plan would look something like this....

#1) The U.S. Congress votes to take back all of the functions that it has delegated to the Federal Reserve and begins to issue debt-free United States Notes. These United States Notes would have the exact same value as existing Federal Reserve Notes, and over time all existing Federal Reserve Notes would be taken out of circulation.

#2) The U.S. Congress nationalizes all debt held by the Federal Reserve. That would instantly reduce the national debt by 1.6 trillion dollars. In fact, there are a few members of Congress that have already proposed this.

#3) A Constitutional amendment is passed limiting future U.S. government deficits to a reasonable percentage of GDP. Any future deficits would not be funded by borrowing. Rather, future deficits would be funded by newly created Federal Reserve Notes. Therefore, the federal government would never again accumulate another penny of debt.

And it would be important to inject new money into the economy from time to time. When existing money is destroyed or when the population grows it is important to inject a certain amount of new money into the system in order to avoid deflation.

#4) The existing national debt would be very slowly paid off with newly created United States Notes. The U.S. government spent over 454 billion dollars on interest on the national debt during fiscal year 2011, and over time this expense would go to zero.

If the national debt is paid off slowly enough, it would not create too much inflation. I believe that it could be paid off gradually over 50 years without shocking the economy too much.

There are some that would object to any measure that would ever cause a small amount of inflation, but my contention is that we have created a $15 trillion dollar debt mess for future generations, and it would be absolutely criminal to pass that legacy on to them.

We created this mess, and it is our responsibility to clean it up.

While there is certainly a danger that we would have a limited amount of inflation under a debt-free monetary system such as the one described above, the reality is that we are absolutely guaranteed inflation under the Federal Reserve system.

Most Americans believe that inflation is a fact of life, but the sad truth is that the United States has only had a major, ongoing problem with inflation since the Federal Reserve was created back in 1913.

If you do not believe this, just check out this chart.

Sadly, the U.S. dollar has lost well over 95 percent of its value since the Federal Reserve was created.

So, yes, there would be a need for strict monetary discipline under a debt-free monetary system, but it would be hard to do worse than the Federal Reserve has already been doing.

And Congress could always slow down inflation using other methods. For example, raising the reserve requirements for banks (which should be done anyway) would help keep inflation in check.

If the above proposals were adopted, the end result would be something that we could all live with. The Federal Reserve system would be abolished, the national debt burden on future generations would be wiped out, the economy would not have to go through a devastating economic collapse that could last a decade or longer, and we could eventually make a fairly smooth transition to "hard money" if we wanted to after the national debt is gone.

Is there any other proposal out there that does all of those things?

There are many out there that would dispute some of the points above, and debate is good. By engaging in debate, we can hopefully help educate the American people about the nature of money.

The key is to get rid of our current debt-based Federal Reserve Notes and replace them with debt-free United States Notes.

The American people need to understand that it is a lie that the U.S. government "must" borrow money from somebody else.

When the U.S. government borrows money, it slowly transfers wealth from the American people to those that borrowed it.

At this point, we have created a financial nightmare for future generations that is unlike anything the world has ever seen before. We owe it to future generations to eliminate the debt problem without destroying the United States economy. Adopting debt-free money would allow us to do that.

But sadly, neither political party is even talking about debt-free money. In fact, most of the politicians in both political parties probably do not even know what debt-free money is.

So we need to get the American people educated about these things. Because if we stay on the course that we are currently on, an economic collapse is inevitable.

Aldo Moro

Law 31-3-1966 n. 171

The Chamber of Deputies and the Senate of the Republic have approved;

THE PRESIDENT OF THE REPUBLIC

PROMULGATES

the following law:
Article 1.

The manufacture and issue of 500 lire state notes is authorised.
With decrees of the President of the Republic, upon proposal of the Minister for the Treasury, the characteristics and quotas of the tickets themselves will be determined.
The date from which the notes referred to in this law will have legal tender status, and the limit for their redeeming power, will be established by decree of the Minister for the Treasury.

Article 2.

The Minister for the Treasury is authorized to stipulate specific agreements with the Bank of Italy to regulate all relationships arising from the implementation of this law between the State Treasury and the issuing institution, as well as to contribute, with own decrees, any budget changes.

This law, bearing the seal of the State, will be included in the official collection of laws and decrees of the Italian Republic. Whoever is responsible for observing it and ensuring it is observed as state law is obliged.

Given in Rome, 31 March 1966

SARAGAT

MORO - COLOMBO

Seen, the Keeper of the Seals: REALE

Original in Italian:

Legge 31-3-1966 n. 171

La Camera dei deputati ed il Senato della Repubblica hanno approvato;

IL PRESIDENTE DELLA REPUBBLICA

PROMULGA

la seguente legge:

Art. 1.

E' autorizzata la fabbricazione e l'emissione di biglietti di Stato da lire 500. Con decreti del Presidente della Repubblica, su proposta del Ministro per il tesoro, saranno determinate le caratteristiche ed i contingenti dei biglietti stessi.

La data dalla quale i biglietti di cui alla presente legge avranno corso legale, ed il limite per il loro potere liberatorio, saranno stabiliti con decreto del Ministro per il tesoro.

Art. 2.

Il Ministro per il tesoro e' autorizzato a stipulare apposite convenzioni con la Banca d'Italia per regolare tutti i rapporti nascenti, dall'attuazione della presente legge, tra il Tesoro dello Stato e l'Istituto di emissione, nonche' ad apportare, con propri decreti, le eventuali variazioni di bilancio.

La presente legge, munita del sigillo dello Stato, sara' inserta nella Raccolta ufficiale delle leggi e dei decreti della Repubblica italiana. E' fatto obbligo a chiunque spetti di osservarla e di farla osservare come legge dello Stato.

Data a Roma, addi' 31 marzo 1966

SARAGAT

MORO - COLOMBO

Visto, il Guardasigilli: REALE

INDEX

Bibliography on the accounting of bank money creation

Prof. Massimo Costa, *On the accounting nature of "monetary liabilities" in bank balance sheets*, ed. RIREA, June 2009 - http://www.rirea.it/rirea/node/214

Prof. Charles W. Mulford, Eugene E. Comiskey, *Cash Flow Reporting by Financial Companies: A Look at the Commercial Banks*, Georgia Tech College of Management, July 2009 - https://smartech.gatech.edu/handle/1853/29098

Michael Schemmann CPA, *Accounting Perversion in Bank Financial Statements*: Root Cause of the Ongoing Global Financial Crisis, 2012
https://www.amazon.com/Accounting-Perversion-Bank-Financial-Statements/dp/1468171119

Prof. Asgeir B. Torfason, *Cash flow accounting in banks – a study of practice*, University of Gothenburg, April 2014. https://gupea.ub.gu.se/handle/2077/35272

Prof. Antonino Galloni, *The future of the bank - Outlines of banking and financial theory*, ed. Eurilink, August 2014
http://eurilink.it/prodotti/il-futuro-della-banca-lineamenti-di-teoria-bancaria-e-finanziaria-2/

Thomas Mayer, Roman Huber, *Vollgeld: Das Geldsystem der Zukunft*. Our article from the Financial Report Taschenbuch, Tectum Sachbuch, August 2014
https://www.amazon.de/Vollgeld-Geldsystem-Zukunft-Unser-Finanzkrise/dp/3828833500

EFRAG, *Statement of Cash Flows: issues for Financial Institutions*, 2015
https://www.efrag.org/Activities/335/Statement-of-Cash-Flows-issues-for-Financial-Institutions

Michael Schemmann CPA, *Putting a Stop to Fictitious Bank Accounting*, 2015
https://www.amazon.com/Putting-Stop-Fictitious-Bank-Accounting/dp/1511593598

Prof. Richard A. Werner, *A lost century in economics: Three theories of banking and the conclusive evidence*, International Review of Financial Analysis
Volume 46, July 2016, Pages 361-379
https://www.sciencedirect.com/science/article/pii/S1057521915001477

Prof. Dirk J. BEZEMER - *Towards an 'accounting view' on money, banking and the macroeconomy: history, empirics, theory*, Cambridge Journal of Economics, Volume 40, Issue 5, pp. 1275-1295, September 2016
https://academic.oup.com/cje/article-abstract/40/5/1275/1987682

Marco Della Luna, *SCRIPTURAL MONEY: THE ORDERS OF THE COURT*, 28 February 2017 - http://marcodellaluna.info/sito/2017/02/28/moneta-scritturale-le-ordinanze-del-tribunale/

Silvio Orlandi, *A journey through the non-bank loan. Critical analysis of the monetary issue*, Sindimedia Edizioni, May 2018 - https://www.amazon.it/viaggio-attraverso-bancario-questione-monetaria/dp/883199400X

Biagio Bossone, Massimo Costa, *The "accounting view" of money: money as equity*, The World Bank, May 2018 - http://blogs.worldbank.org/allaboutfinance/accounting-view-money-money-equity-part-i

Bossone, B.; Costa, M.; Cuccia, A.; Valenza, G. *Accounting Meets Economics: Towards an 'Accounting View' of Money* - 2018 https://papers.ssrn.com/sol3/papers.cfm?abstract_id=3270860

Zhan Gao, Weijia Li, John O'Hanlon, *The informativeness of U.S. banks' statements of cash flows*, Journal of Accounting Literature, Volume 43, December 2019, pp. 1-18 https://www.sciencedirect.com/science/article/pii/S0737460718300624

Michael Kumhof, Jason Allen, Will Bateman, Rosa Lastra, Simon Gleeson, Saule Omarova, *Central Bank Money: Liability, Asset, or Equity of the Nation?* - Cornell Law School research paper No. 20-46, 5 August 2020 https://papers.ssrn.com/sol3/papers.cfm?abstract_id=3730608

The finances of European liberation: with particular reference to Italy - Frank A, Southard, ed. Italian: 2021 - https://www.amazon.it/finanze-della-liberazione-europea-particolare-ebook/dp/B08YK23B6J

Biagio Bossone, *BANKING SEIGNORAGE IN AN ECONOMY OF MONEY PRODUCTION, POST-KEYNESIAN ECONOMICS SOCIETY* - August 2021 https://centralerischibanche.blogspot.com/2021/11/il-signoraggio-bancario-in-uneconomia.html

De Gruyter - *Money for the Issuer: Liability or Equity?* - Economics 2021; 15:43-59 - Research article - Bossone and Costa - https://doi.org/10.1515/econ-2021-0004

Biagio Bossone, *Bank Money Creation and the Payments System* - PKES Working Paper 2117 - November 2021 - https://www.postkeynesian.net/working-papers/2117/

The Law of Central Bank Reserve Creation, Will Bateman & Jason Allen, Modern Law Review, March 2022 https://www.modernlawreview.co.uk/march-2022/law-central-bank-reserve-creation/

Synopsis:

Ezra Pound and Giacinto Auriti, the Poet and the Peasant Jurist. Apparently different characters, by origin and culture, but united by an indissoluble bond: the search for the truth at all costs. Ezra Pound asks five questions that no one has ever answered: Money, Credit, Interest, Usury and Circulation; Auriti gives, in this essay, precise answers. An ideal continuity that unites them in the school of heretical economists. Auriti elaborates the new theory of value "as a relationship between phases of time" which will lead him to the discovery of the "induced value" of money. "Those who create the value of money are not those who print it but the people who accept it as a means of payment", however, it is the bankers, the great usurers, who appropriate the monetary value, using it as an instrument of domination and imposing on humanity the seigniorage of debt. And here is the ingenious solution to the problem: Popular ownership of money, which returns to the people the ill-gotten gains of the monetary values that it creates. The hope is that governments will manage the monetary issue and distribute the profits, as a citizen's income, to all citizens.

More books by the same editor:
https://www.amazon.it/stores/author/B0854KRSMQ

www.ingramcontent.com/pod-product-compliance
Lightning Source LLC
Chambersburg PA
CBHW060004300526
45794CB00003B/1083